I0116672

Nuclear Japan

Kanji Ishizumi

Grosvenor House
Publishing Limited

All rights reserved
Copyright © Kanji Ishizumi, 2022

The right of Kanji Ishizumi to be identified as the author of this
work has been asserted in accordance with Section 78
of the Copyright, Designs and Patents Act 1988

The book cover is copyright to Kanji Ishizumi

This book is published by
Grosvenor House Publishing Ltd
Link House
140 The Broadway, Tolworth, Surrey, KT6 7HT.
www.grosvenorhousepublishing.co.uk

This book is sold subject to the conditions that it shall not, by way of
trade or otherwise, be lent, resold, hired out or otherwise circulated
without the author's or publisher's prior consent in any form of binding or
cover other than that in which it is published and
without a similar condition including this condition being imposed
on the subsequent purchaser.

A CIP record for this book
is available from the British Library

ISBN 978-1-83975-796-9

A nuclear-armed Japan:

A vital element in the West's confrontation with China and Russia

Introduction

The following pages reflect my concerns about the present state of Japan and how the country could secure a viable future. I do not dwell on the ideas of economists, valuable as they may be to a degree. A country's true prosperity is not forged by the fine-sounding words of such people, which often focus too much on theory while ignoring people's actual circumstances.

And what is the reality of the situation we in Japan face? There is the saying "The wise man learns from history but the fool is governed by the present." We adherents of Judaism have learned through our studies of the Torah (the Five Books of Moses) that if our attention is consumed by the minutiae of today, tomorrow or yesterday, we cannot perceive the truth. It is my hope through these pages to impart to my readers the historical reality of what constitutes real national prosperity and therefore what statesmen should do to bring it about.

It is worth repeating that human history is the history of war. However much people may yearn for peace, there is no escaping the fact that war has been a constant factor in our evolution. And in order to prevail in wars, people have continuously sought after and developed ever more powerful weapons. One could say that arms have been at the heart of the vicissitudes experienced by all tribes and races. The ancient Hittite kingdom, with its iron weapons, vanquished the neighbouring peoples who bore only bronze arms with the ease of a knife cutting through butter and came to dominate Mesopotamia. Meanwhile, Assyria, which had forged a great empire in Mesopotamia in the pre-Christian era, boasting the most powerful arms of the era, overwhelmed the peoples of the surrounding regions through its heavily-armed cavalry, engineers and siege forces. The Scythians, using composite bows far more lethal than their traditional counterparts, powerful new weapons which could be fired from horseback, dominated the Iranian plateau and extended their power to Egypt. Genghis Khan built his Mongolian Empire with his reinforced composite bows together with arrows and arrowheads featuring immense precision. The Byzantine Empire, with its warships equipped with flame throwers, was able to keep its enemies away from its capital, Constantinople. In medieval Europe, the quality of the cannons wielded by different countries had a great bearing on their relative prosperity.

Thus, competition to develop armaments has led to the emergence in the present era of "weapons of mass destruction". These devices, including biological, chemical and nuclear arms, have the power to inflict devastating harm on both people and buildings. There is no doubt that such weapons are inhumane and capable of causing indiscriminate slaughter that would have been unimaginable in the past. On the other hand, it is also true that they have been brought into being through human will.

Among armaments of mass destruction, nuclear weapons have particular significance. Whereas chemical and biological weapons were outlawed as inhumane by the Geneva Protocol of 1925, the use of nuclear weapons, even though they are likewise inhumane weapons of mass destruction, had never been banned under the Treaty on the Prohibition of Nuclear Weapons until it entered into force on 22 January 2021. However, the reality is that the Treaty is no more than just a declaration of principle by the non-nuclear states. It is a fact that Singapore, The Netherlands, all of the nuclear-armed nations and all NATO members, as well as Saudi Arabia, Egypt, Syria, Jordan, the UAE and other Gulf nations such as Bahrain, Kuwait and Qatar, Israel, Iran, North and South Korea, Japan and Norway have one thing in common: they have not signed up to the Treaty. Why is that? It boils down to the fact that the countries that possess nuclear weapons have the corresponding ability to actually use them in the future. Thus, those nuclear-armed states make their presence felt in the world militarily and economically by fomenting an atmosphere of "nuclear terror". This can be seen through the global hegemony wielded up to now by America, the first country to develop nuclear weapons.

But it is not only America. Many will recall scenes in 2017 of French President Emmanuel Macron being lowered onto the deck on one his country's nuclear-powered submarines clad in military attire. And why did Macron broadcast that scene to the world? It was to let everyone know that France had a nuclear-powered submarine capable of launching ballistic missiles. With France unable to make its presence felt on a par with the other permanent members of the UN Security Council and feeling itself in the shadow of Germany in the EU, it is impossible to ignore the fact that what gives it its international influence as a "great power" is its possession of nuclear weapons.

Of course, it is not just a matter of nuclear-armed states exerting their influence. They have taken it upon themselves to attack, devastate and chronically weaken those without atomic weapons, turning them into vassal states. The Japanese people need to realise that this is the reality of the post-Second World War order. Such countries as Vietnam, Afghanistan, Iraq, Libya and Syria attest to this fact. These countries have all suffered attacks with overwhelming force by America or Russia.

As for how incredibly easily a non-nuclear state can be overwhelmed by one with atomic weapons, one need only look to Russia's invasion of Ukraine as recently as in 2014. As part of the former Soviet Union, Ukraine was where roughly one-third of the Soviet nuclear arsenal was stored. However, following the collapse of the Soviet Union, Ukraine either abolished its nuclear armaments or transferred them to Russia, voluntarily becoming a non-nuclear power. One can surmise that, if Ukraine had not abandoned nuclear weapons or had retained just a few of them, Russia would not have taken over Crimea nor could it have threatened to invade eastern Ukraine.

These thoughts prompted me to take a look at the history of two cities. This was because of the striking contrast in their fortunes.

One of them was conspicuous by its military might, possessing impressive munitions production facilities and a large quantity of warships and weapons. It may well have been the pre-eminent military power in mediaeval Europe. It was a mercantile city whose commercial reach extended to the Near and Middle East. Until it fell to Napoleon's forces, not once did it suffer aggression or find itself at the mercy of another country.

The other city, occupying a strategic position on the trade route linking the Silk Road and the Mediterranean Sea, was a commercial city with a long history stretching from about 2000 BC to the present century and boasting a level of prosperity unparalleled in the Middle East. However, as this city never had a strong army or the most powerful weapons of the age, it was constantly invaded by Mesopotamia, a proud military power. In ancient times there were the Hittites, the Assyrians, the invading Huns from Central Asia, Alexander the Great, and the Byzantine and Ottoman empires. The city of which we speak was scorned by these great powers and, in the present day, has been completely destroyed, its citizens scattered with nowhere to live.

The first of these two cities was Venice; the other Aleppo.

They both boasted historically high levels of prosperity, but their destinies were very different. While in the present day Venice flourishes as an historical tourism destination, Aleppo has been utterly laid to waste, with few traces of its glorious past.

Aleppo used to be Syria's largest city, with a population of 2.5 million. It was of such historical significance that it was made a UNESCO World Heritage Site. As for why such a prosperous Middle Eastern city repeatedly came under the sway of other powers for 1,000 and even 2,000 years and why Venice survived unscathed, history demonstrates the importance of a country being strong enough to prevent its destruction by others.

It must be the case that, if modern Syria had possessed nuclear weapons, its government troops would have crushed the rebels, Aleppo would have avoided the devastation it suffered and its citizens would have been able to continue to enjoy living in a city with its exalted international status. In short, history teaches us that enduring prosperity is impossible without powerful armaments.

The course that Venice followed contrasted greatly with that of Aleppo. In short, it was a city built on military power.

Although people view it these days as a tourist destination, from the 12th century onwards until the eve of the Industrial Revolution it was Europe's pre-eminent military-industrial state. It specialised in producing weapons and warships, and for more than 700 years manufactured armaments boasting the greatest destructive power in Europe.

Let us consider an example of its prowess in this regard. In 1593 the famous Galileo Galilei was appointed the Minister of Engineering of Venice. He proposed what were considered at the time to be the most cutting-edge methods of producing weapons and advised on maximising their destructive power. Galileo involved himself in the development of various kinds of armaments but devoted particular attention to studying ballistics. This is the study of how an object is propelled into the air with a certain amount of power, the trajectory it follows and where it comes to rest. Thus, by calculating backwards the force of the object at the time it reaches its target, Galileo was able to shed light on how to make the sides of warships more resistant to projectiles fired at them. He also gave his attention to improving the performance of oars so as to increase the propulsion power of ships, with the result that the vessels he designed boasted the highest propulsion and speed of any at the time. At its peak Venice was a formidable naval power, with 3,000 merchant ships and 3,000 warships, totalling 6,000 vessels. It vied with the Ottoman Empire for dominance over the Mediterranean Sea.

Venice's prosperity was guaranteed by its awesome military power and its possession of the largest munitions factory in mediaeval Europe. By contrast, Aleppo was periodically oppressed and dominated by the military might of more powerful countries. Does not present-day Japan, subordinate to America and bound by the requirements of the Japan-US Security Treaty, have something in common with Aleppo at that time? And it should not be forgotten that the definitive conclusion for Aleppo was the destruction of the city. The tragedy of Aleppo was the tragedy of countries that do not have nuclear weapons. Could we hope that sometime in the future Tokyo will be guaranteed not to become another Aleppo?

In a sense one could lump together America with China, Russia and North Korea. If one takes a look at the countries surrounding Japan, they largely comprise those with nuclear weapons. By contrast, Japan openly declares that it has not organised nuclear shelters and, in accordance with the Three Non-Nuclear Principles, has no intention of acquiring nuclear weapons. One could say that this puts Japan at the mercy of an opponent who could attack we know not when.

On 12 June 2018, former US President Donald Trump met Kim Jong-un, head of the Korean Workers' Party and Supreme Leader of North Korea, for a summit in Singapore. It was an historic occasion marking the first ever meeting between the heads of the two countries, and the wild enthusiasm with which if was greeted around the world is still fresh in the memory.

However, could North Korea really be expected to abandon its nuclear weapons? Manuel Noriega of Panama, Saddam Hussein of Iraq and Muammar Gaddafi of Libya, all of them dictators without nuclear weapons, had been overthrown by nuclear-armed America. Aware of those events, Kim Jong-un would have little reason to easily abolish his nuclear weapons. And even supposing that he did so, it is highly likely that he would still have long-range ballistic missiles that could reach America and medium-range ballistic missiles capable of threatening Japan. And as for present-day North Korea, if it did not have a nuclear capability, how could it earn foreign exchange? It is because it possesses nuclear weapons that it is able to sell nuclear technology to the likes of Iran; if that were not the case, its foreign-currency income would disappear, leading to its complete collapse. However, if, for argument's sake, North Korea abandoned all its nuclear weapons, how much of a relief would that actually be? Clearly, it is not Russia, which occupies Japan's Northern Territories, but China that poses a real and imminent threat to Japan. It is China's military ambition to dominate the South China Sea, and in the East China Sea it aims to control Taiwan.

I have long been warning that the ability of Chinese aircraft carriers to patrol the Pacific freely in the area close to Japan represents a great threat to our country. And yet in recent years the Japanese administration wasted political capital on the meaningless goal of trying to reform the constitution. In order to deter China's malevolent military ambitions, it is imperative to seriously consider establishing a security set-up encompassing the expansion of the Self-Defence Forces both physically and institutionally, and in particular acquiring nuclear weapons. Having as an enemy a country boasting a population of 1.3 billion including young people who can serve in the armed forces, a country which is thus overwhelmingly superior in terms of human capital as well as land and natural resources and also possesses the newest and most powerful nuclear weapons, Japan needs to furnish itself with armaments of equivalent strength.

And yet we are wondering what kind of defence set-up is possible under Article 9 of the current constitution. We need to stop the idiotic wastage of our people's energy in such fruitless pursuits. There is absolutely no question that, rather than worrying about changing the constitution, Japan must acquire the ability to defend itself with nuclear weapons.

The point of this book is not just to argue for the role of war in a country's prosperity. It is rather to declare that Japan's possession of the newest and most powerful weapons sufficient at least to convince a potential aggressor that attacking it will result in its own destruction is not just linked to our country's defence but is an absolute condition for its prosperity.

To develop, possess and deploy weapons that can surpass or at least not fall behind the capacity of rivals is one of the most important factors contributing to the prosperity of any country.

To be blunt, as can be seen from the example of Venice, a country's prosperity is linked with the "science" of its armaments development. This fact, as attested to by history, is what I want to make clear in these pages. Moreover, the science of which I speak here is rooted in fact. This was the case when Japan waged war on America. However, Japan should beware of being motivated by exceptionally emotional factors. If its actions are governed simply by the sense that America will protect it with nuclear weapons based on the group security that binds them, it will be the only country to employ such blind trust. If we take a reasonably cool-headed look at the facts, will we not come to realise precisely what Japan should do?

Based on this conviction, I have realised the foolishness of ignoring the science and pursuing constitutional reform based on meaningless imperialistic idealism, and strongly advocate the necessity of preparing nuclear shelters, building aircraft carriers, and developing nuclear missiles and submarines armed with them.

Chapter 1

The international situation and Japan's position

A strategic proposal concerning security

My proposal regarding Japan's security is as follows:

1 The preparation of nuclear shelters to adequately protect the people – particularly in the Tokyo metropolitan area as well as Osaka and the surrounding region, which could be targets. Then, the creation as quickly as possible of nuclear shelters from which, once the nuclear fallout following an attack has dissipated, retaliatory strikes can be launched.

2 Joining NATO as soon as possible, equipping ourselves with an adequate number of American atomic bombs and nuclear warheads while readying ourselves for actual war.

3 In the event that that joining NATO is not feasible, expeditiously switching the roughly ¥1 trillion per year spent on maintaining the US military presence in Japan to funding our own nuclear programme and preparing domestically the appropriate number of atomic warheads and bombs. Of course, for us to have the necessary retaliatory capability, having our own submarines equipped with nuclear missiles will be indispensable.

To be blunt, what I wish to affirm is that there is no connection between Japan's security and the reform of its constitution. Revising the constitution is not a means of demonstrating the martial spirit of our Self Defence Forces personnel. For the Japanese people, there is nothing untoward about the concept of a pre-emptive attack on enemy territory. Under the present constitution, there is absolutely no problem about having a nuclear weapons capacity for our defence. Moreover, a pre-emptive strike for the purpose of self-defence when the enemy has not yet launched an attack would be consistent with the constitution. I really want to emphasise this point to those people who argue that a nuclear-armed Japan would violate Article 9 of the constitution. What I fear is that, under the pretext of constitutional reform, right-wing ideology might become more prevalent, which could expose Japan to even greater danger than the nuclear threat posed by North Korea.

I am also addressing these words to people who think that Japan will be protected by being under the "nuclear umbrella" provided by the Japan-US Security Treaty. There is absolutely nothing which guarantees that young Americans will sacrifice themselves to defend Japan. It does not bear asking how long the Japanese people can look forward to prosperity without nuclear weapons while entrusting their defence to others. It is just fantasy to suppose that the destruction that befell Aleppo, without cutting-edge arms to defend itself, will not also be visited upon the Japanese people.

Japan's postwar security guarantee was built on the illusion that the country would be protected by the American "nuclear umbrella". However, history teaches us that it takes only a single document to break a treaty between two countries, and the Japan-US Security Treaty comprises just such a document.

The lecture "Constructing a new Japan", which Kanji Ishihara, whom I very much admire, delivered shortly after the end of World War II, includes the following insights:

2

"The ultimate war that will occur following World War II will be fundamentally different from that conflict, where land, sea and air forces were used, and there will be nothing wrong with Japan having turned away from the use of combined forces. The next conflict, what might be called the Third World War, will be a scientific war, different from World Wars I and II when large amounts of equipment and substantial personnel were mobilised, and will be carried out to its conclusion with the ultimate powerful weapons developed by scientists in laboratories. For this reason, in this postwar era Japan needs to value its scientists and to place its hope on them conducting the necessary research and development on the most advanced armaments.

"The reconstruction of Japan needs to realise the highest civilisation based on science and technology. These are the basis of a country's power and can be brought to fulfilment by great discoveries stemming from human endeavour in laboratories. Science and technology are the overriding factors in a country's military power."

Following World War II, the Showa Emperor Hirohito said in a letter to his son, the Heisei Emperor Akihito: "Let me say something about the cause of our defeat. The Japanese people believed too much in our Empire and came to despise Britain and the United States. We put too much weight on spiritual things and forgot about science."

Thus in modern times there is no denying the fact that the most cutting-edge and powerful armaments brought into being by science comprise nuclear weapons. To safeguard the lives and wealth of the Japanese people, one must explore every possible means. As for countries displaying an aggressive attitude, it is necessary to acquire weapons superior to theirs. When it comes to nuclear armaments, Japan too needs to have them for its own protection.

Could Japan intercept a North Korean missile?

So far, in order to guarantee its security, in military terms Japan has consistently given priority to improving its air defence capability. Recently the Japanese government, seeking to prepare for a missile attack by North Korea, which shows no sign of desisting from weapons tests, and realising it ought to equip its forces with a proper interception capability, sought to acquire the Aegis Ashore land-based version of the original Aegis system but, finally realising it had shortcomings as a means for interception, cancelled the order.

In August 2017 a medium-range missile fired by North Korea passed over Hokkaido and landed in the Pacific Ocean. At that time the Japanese government announced that, as it had judged the missile would not fall on Japan, it had not ordered the Self Defence Forces to take action to intercept it. But was that really true? After the government issued its warning to the people, if we consider that there would be only around two minutes before the missile fell into the Pacific Ocean, it is clear that the Self Defence Forces would not be able to shoot it down.

I am extremely pessimistic as, even if Japan's Self-Defence Forces had vessels equipped with the American Sea-Based Aegis Missile Defence System, superior to anything else in existence, North Korea would be able to fire one or more of its many ballistic missiles. What convinces me in this regard is, firstly, that, at the time North Korea fired its missiles, the Aegis-equipped ships would have to be deployed in an appropriate area of the ocean, and that, secondly, the most pressing issue, in the event that North Korea fired dozens of missiles at the same time, in one attack an Aegis vessel would use up all of its interceptor missiles. In such an event the vessel would be forced to return immediately to Sasebo or Yokosuka, install more missiles and set sail again. However, if this situation repeated itself, there is the concern that all of the interceptor missiles at the disposal of the US and Japan would be used up.

This is because, in order to be effective, it would take several interceptor missiles to respond to one attempted strike. Interceptor missiles are extremely expensive and it would be financially impossible to prepare an inexhaustible supply of them. In short, one could imagine a situation in which it became impossible to respond to a North Korean attack with multiple missiles. Thus, it is unrealistic to suppose that our interceptor missiles could guarantee total defence against a missile attack by North Korea.

In the American nuclear defence strategy, the development of interceptor missiles amounts to a kind of insurance for the worst eventuality. But, to be honest, such an approach is hardly reliable. In the US case there is the option of a pre-emptive strike on an enemy base. That is to say, when its much-vaunted intelligence service had inklings that the enemy was about to launch a missile, before that happened the US would be prepared to attack its base with missiles or bombs dropped by its aircraft. As an option open to the US and Japan (if America acted on the provisions of its security agreement with Japan), the US would have to simultaneously fire dozens of Tomahawk missiles deployed in the waters near North Korea and destroy that country's missile base or achieve the same result with the use of B-2 stealth bombers that cannot be detected by radar. However, it is entirely possible that even America's most powerful 30,000lb bombs would not be able to take out the underground missile bases that North Korea has persisted in building. Moreover, it would be impossible to detect in advance the movements of North Korean missiles launched from mobile bases or submarines.

Whatever the case may be, if the US Army found itself in this situation, the North Korean terrestrial forces would swarm into South Korea, consisting of one million regular soldiers and six million auxiliaries. This action would engulf not just Seoul but the whole of the South in war. And if we consider American military personnel and their families left in South Korea, the US would inevitably vacillate and would probably be unable to take the appropriate action.

Moreover, as for North Korea, if its forces advanced on the South the latter's army could be expected to retaliate, and the hostilities would continue until one of the parties collapsed. Such a risk would be difficult for either the North or the South to contemplate. Thus, the lowest hurdle towards military action by North Korea would consist of an attack on Japan. And if Japan stumbled into initiating a pre-emptive strike on an enemy base, it would invite retaliation from multiple North Korean missiles hidden in undersea and underground locations. In short, one could well imagine the circumstances in which Japan became the victim of a North Korean missile attack.

China and its domination of the South China Sea

Although we have so far focused exclusively on the North Korean nuclear issue, in essence there seems no room for doubt that the greatest threat facing Japan is China. It does not hide its sinister intention of replacing America as the regional hegemon and its defence budget is rising steadily.

In April 2017 its first domestically-produced aircraft carrier, *Shandong*, entered service. As well as now having two aircraft carriers, China is building a third and a fourth. It will soon have six 100,000-tonne class destroyers. One could say that China has become a genuine naval power, surpassing Russia and ranking second only to America with its 11 aircraft carriers. Moreover, it is investing vast amounts in its military and, as well as procuring cutting-edge hardware such as Su-35 fighter aircraft and the S400 ground-to-air missile system from

Russia, it is continuing to upgrade its capabilities by launching volume production of its own J-20 stealth fighter.

As a particularly urgent matter, in the East China Sea Chinese ships constantly encroach into the area around the Senkaku islands, owned by Japan, making no secret of Beijing's territorial ambitions, but the real aim is to dominate the sea in the vicinity of those islands (through Anti-Access/Area Denial, or A2/AD) as a means of threatening Japan in the event of a Chinese attack on Taiwan. Of course, at its missile base in Manchuria, China has installed nuclear ballistic missiles aimed at major Japanese cities and US bases in Japan. Moreover, having consolidated its control of Hong Kong, China has as its next strategy the annexation of Taiwan.

Meanwhile, China is seeking to extend its reach without any constraints from the East China Sea, where Japan and the US forces in Okinawa are on the alert, to the South China Sea, through its Anti-Access/Area Denial (A2/AD) strategy. In simple terms, A2/AD amounts to preventing an opponent from approaching, traversing or carrying out any offensive action in a particular area. As opposed to a legalistic view of a country's airspace or territorial waters, it involves the actual military dominance of the air or the sea in the relevant region. For instance, although the Senkaku islands belong to Japan from a legal point of view, if China were to adopt an A2/AD strategy in the area, that would be the end of the matter. China's hurried construction of military bases in the Spratly and Paracel Islands is for this purpose. America sometimes sends naval vessels to the vicinity of the islands to assert its right of "Freedom of Navigation", but the truth is that China has already applied its A2/AD doctrine virtually throughout the South China Sea.

The main reason why China places so much store on establishing an A2/AD regime in the South China Sea is to create a scenario of "mutually assured destruction" vis-à-vis America. It is a plot to take effective control of the area around the islands and turn it into a fortress and to deploy nuclear-powered submarines equipped with atomic warheads. Although one purpose is for those submarines to sail through the Bashi Channel into the Pacific and to target the American mainland, an equally important goal is to have in its sights what for China is the eyesore of the US Forces in Okinawa. This is because, in the South China Sea, the most important body of water for China, Okinawa represents an obstacle to everything China wants to do. It really stands in the way of the mainstay vessels of the Chinese fleet as they leave their mother ports in the Shandong or Liaodong peninsula and make their way into the Pacific. Or to put it another way, as I will make clear later, from the viewpoint of the overall security of Japan and the US, Okinawa could be said to be a lifeline. It is true that the US military, naturally, as well as the Japanese Self-Defence Forces engage in top-secret drills by dispatching submarines to the South China Sea, but it is difficult to counter the dominance in the area of China's nuclear-powered submarines.

Unlike the Senkaku Islands, the South China Sea has a direct bearing on Japan's livelihood. The crude oil brought through the South China Sea in tankers from the Middle East and other goods are absolutely essential for the Japanese economy. Should Japan-China or US-China tensions escalate to a critical level, it is possible that Japanese vessels traversing the area could be seized.

If only Japan had nuclear weapons, China would probably not resort to such reckless behaviour. Unfortunately, however, due to Japan's lack of military strength, its vessels would probably have no option but to make a detour through the Java and Makassar straits and along the East coast of the Philippines, a rough and wild sea for tankers. The accompanying rise in fuel costs and extra time taken would have an impact on the Japanese economy in terms of increased commodity prices. As for China, it would be able to gain a stranglehold on Japan without having to resort to military force.

Moreover, it is not only the South China Sea that is at issue. Japan's dependence on the Middle East for crude oil is around 80%, but what would happen if the Chinese Navy, having advanced into the Indian Ocean, bore down on the Strait of Hormuz? China already has the right to operate in the area through the Port of Gwadar in Pakistan, which is only 400km from the Strait of Hormuz, on the basis of its Belt and Road Initiative. It has denied that it has made Gwadar a naval port, but no credence can be placed on that. Under the guise of carrying out anti-piracy policies, it is already operating a large number of vessels in the Indian Ocean. One could well imagine the scenario in which China and Iran, acting in concert, shut off the Strait of Hormuz. The Quad, an alliance bringing together Japan, the US, Australia and India for a 'Free and Open Indo-Pacific', would not be able to deter them from shutting off the Strait. Furthermore, while China offers generous loans to developing countries, in cases of late repayment it has them agree to allow its long-term use of their ports, so that in the future we can expect to see the number of such ports acting as bases of the Chinese Navy proliferate. If Japan had nuclear weapons and adopted a correspondingly tough stance, it is as clear as day that China's brazen behaviour would change accordingly.

The necessity of nuclear shelters

The critical state of Japan's security makes it indisputable that the country's continued prosperity rests on its possession of nuclear weapons. However, as well as equipping itself with such arms, there is one other thing that Japan needs to pursue. This is the preparation of nuclear shelters. In the present circumstances in which North Korea has nuclear weapons and Japan lacks the means to retaliate, Japan needs to place priority on equipping itself with such shelters. The Venice of yore, as well as being protected by a natural moat in the form of the sea, surrounded itself with high, sturdy walls and was thus adequately sheltered. In the nuclear age, the construction of adequate shelters must be the first step for Japan if it is to emulate Venice.

Currently the only two countries to have installed nuclear shelters for their entire populations are Switzerland and Israel. In Switzerland, nestled in the Alps, many tunnels for motorways have been built in the mountains, all of them equipped to be used as nuclear shelters. Of course, the same thing applies outside mountain areas, with underground shelters also in place. Moreover, as gamma rays, the most permeable form of radiation, can only be blocked by thick metal plates made of lead or iron, in Switzerland it is expressly stipulated that shelters must be built with iron sheets 21cm thick and concrete 66cm thick, and at a depth of more than 1 metre so as to restrict the penetration of gamma rays to no more than 1 part in 1,000.

Meanwhile, in Israel most underground car parks have been designed so that they can be converted into nuclear shelters in an instant. In many hospitals, all of the operating theatres, medical equipment and other items can be transferred to underground nuclear shelters, where they can function normally. Moreover, various school buildings are reinforced with thick concrete and steel walls so that they can be used as nuclear shelters.

In the case of Israel, as one never knows when guerrillas or terrorists from organisations such as Hamas or Hezbollah may gain possession of a small nuclear bomb and launch an attack and, as the risk of a nuclear strike by Iran is high, the government has engaged in the construction of nuclear shelters.

Apart from these two countries, Sweden, which has brought back conscription because of rising concerns about Russia, has installed 65,000 nuclear shelters which can accommodate 81% of the population. At the same time, Finland, which has historically been susceptible to invasion by Russia, has in place shelters that can cover 70% of the population.

Furthermore, Sweden has a garrison on the island of Gotland in the Baltic Sea and has built 350 reinforced nuclear shelters there to ensure the survival of its troops. Thus, a nuclear shelter is not just a place for concealing people but also has the function of enabling the army which evaded a nuclear strike to retaliate.

One reason for the enthusiasm of these countries for constructing nuclear shelters is that they are not members of NATO. That organisation has the strategy of sharing a certain number of American nuclear warheads. Currently around 10 to 20 are stationed in Belgium, approximately 20 in the Netherlands, 20 – 100 in Germany and 50 – 100 in Italy. As for the installed nuclear warheads, the participating countries' bombers are equipped with them in case of emergency and the right to use them resides in the NATO headquarters. Switzerland and Israel are not under any "nuclear umbrella" resulting from such "nuclear sharing" and have no alternative but to rely on themselves for protection. However, it should not be forgotten that members of NATO have on average nuclear shelters covering around 20 – 30 per cent of their populations.

Incidentally, North Korea, a nuclear-armed state, has nuclear shelters that can accommodate the majority of the population. In contrast, Japan, under the Japan-US Security Treaty on which it cannot rely, has virtually none. The Japanese people need to understand the gravity of the situation in which their country is exposed as naked before the nuclear threat from North Korea and, more to the point, the atomic weapons of China and Russia. The fact is that Japan has not joined NATO, has lost faith in the unreliable, empty provisions of the Japan-US Security Treaty, and so far remains unequipped with nuclear shelters. Is this not a huge blunder for which our politicians, particularly those in the Liberal Democratic Party, which has historically enjoyed almost untrammelled power, should be called to account?

In fact, in the face of North Korea's nuclear development and missile launches, the government seems belatedly to have set about the construction of nuclear shelters. This can be seen in the new section of Ring Road No. 2, dubbed the "MacArthur Road", rapidly completed in time for the Tokyo 2020 Olympic Games. Along the MacArthur Road there is a long tunnel running from the Toranomon area to Shimbashi. This tunnel is said to have been built so that it could be used as a spacious nuclear shelter to which the functions of government could be evacuated in an emergency.

Of course, it is important for government functions to continue in such circumstances, but if the majority of the Self-Defence Forces personnel responsible for retaliating as well as of the population at large were wiped out, this would be meaningless. Japan needs to construct nuclear shelters without delay, standing alongside Israel, the pioneer in protecting its citizens from an atomic attack in this way.

To provide nuclear shelters for the entire population would require massive investment. It may well be asked whether Japan has the funds necessary. However, let us think about this. It is said that the planned construction of the linear motor car, which will run from Tokyo to Nagoya and eventually as far as Osaka, will cost around ¥10 trillion. For that amount, how many nuclear shelters could be constructed? When all is said and done, how important is it to be able to get from Tokyo to Osaka in one hour? Is it really worth thinking about at a time when online conferences and teleworking have come to dominate people's working practices because of the coronavirus pandemic?

Membership of NATO

In any discussion of Japan equipping itself with nuclear weapons, we have to take on board the idea of choosing to join NATO as the most realistic means of achieving this. At the heart of this notion is the fundamental difference between the Japan-US Security Treaty and NATO. It is my view that it is worth breaking the bilateral agreement.

On top of there being no third party such as a court that can impose a penalty for breaking a contract, in the case of a treaty, which is a contract between countries, it is a fact that one party can revoke it. As proof of this, is there not the case of the Soviet-Japanese Neutrality Pact that Stalin broke so easily? Indeed, at the time there were fears that the Soviets would occupy not just Manchuria and North Korea but territory as far as Hokkaido.

In contrast, NATO involves a pact among several countries. If one member were to violate it, a penalty could be imposed on it by the other countries, so such a transgression would not be so easy to carry out. Membership of NATO brings with it "nuclear sharing". This is a major difference. There is a big difference between Germany, a member of NATO and a country which has been given nuclear warheads, and Japan, which has not been given them under the Japan-US Security Treaty, in their relative ability to defend themselves with nuclear means. As opposed to Germany, which has a genuine security guarantee, Japan merely has the empty promise of the "nuclear umbrella" provided by the Japan-US Security Treaty.

The wording "North Atlantic Treaty Organisation" may prompt some people to doubt whether Japan, given its Pacific location, might be able to join, but the idea is by no means absurd. The purpose of NATO when it was set up in 1949 was for its member states to cooperate in defending themselves from military threats, particularly nuclear attacks, from the then-Soviet Union, and the same thing apples vis-à-vis Russia today. Thus, there should be no obstacle to the participation of Japan, which could well be the target of a nuclear attack by Russia.

In fact, German Chancellor Merkel is reported to have proposed to then-PM Abe in 2015 that Japan join NATO. Moreover, in July 2019 the Japanese Government set up a NATO liaison section at its Embassy in Brussels, Belgium, where the NATO Headquarters is based. So far Japan has cooperated with NATO on such matters as peacekeeping activities and anti-piracy policies, and this action of the government seems to be aimed at strengthening the links.

Japan has traditionally lined up with European countries in confronting Russia. The Anglo-Japanese Alliance signed in 1902 had exactly that aim. In the 1890s our two countries worked together in facing up to Russia's aggressive intentions on the world stage, Britain in the West and Japan in the East. In the Russo-Japanese war fought in the Sea of Japan, the fact that our combined fleet was able to crush Imperial Russia's Baltic Fleet owes much to the cooperation extended by Britain. Meanwhile, in the First World War Japan played a direct role in European security. The Imperial Navy sent a squadron to the Mediterranean Sea, where they made a major contribution by taking part in action against the German U-boats with the loss of 72 personnel.

Prior to the Second World War, Japan this time joined forces with Germany to pin down the Soviet forces and thus was deeply involved in events concerning Europe. In 1936 the Anti-Comintern Pact was signed between Japan and Germany and was extended the following year to include Italy, becoming the Tripartite Pact in 1940. Although this arrangement was ostensibly aimed at the US and Britain, in essence it involved Germany and Japan collaborating in a pincer movement against their common enemy, the Soviet Union. Thus it was that, when Stalin realised the Japanese Kwantung Army in Manchuria was not going to encroach on Soviet territory, that knowledge helped him in planning his advance into Europe. Taking part in such an agreement turned out to be a bad move for Japan but, as we can see from history, Japan has become essential for Europe in its confrontation with Russia.

In these circumstances, NATO's smaller members may well feel troubled at getting involved with conflicts not involving Russia, that is to say with North Korea or China. However, core members Britain and Germany would probably not object to Japan's participation. If these two countries gave their approval, it would be difficult for France to oppose it. Moreover, America would probably welcome it from a financial viewpoint. And if these three countries approved Japan's membership, it should not be difficult to persuade the smaller countries waiting on the sidelines to do so too.

But could Japan actually join NATO? In fact, there would be no need to revise Article 5. Whether it be New Zealand or Japan, even countries outside the North Atlantic region can join NATO. If Japan were to become a member, of course the treaty would be revised. Article 5 stipulates as follows:

"The Parties agree that an armed attack against one or more of them in Europe or North America shall be considered an attack against them all and consequently they agree that, if such an armed attack occurs, each of them, in exercise of the right of individual or collective self-defence recognised by Article 51 of the Charter of the United Nations, will assist the Party or Parties so attacked by taking forthwith, individually and in concert with the other Parties, such action as it deems necessary, including the use of armed force, to restore and maintain the security of the North Atlantic area."

Japan's participation could be permitted if the words "in Europe or North America" were removed from the above text. The term "the right of collective self-defence", domestically and according to Article 9 of our constitution, would imply the authority to resist an attack. However, as I outline later, the right of collective self-defence is entirely in accordance with the constitution and not only in the light of the revision to the security law enacted in 2015. Externally, as it does not violate the Non-Proliferation Treaty, the issue of Japan attracting international criticism does not arise. Could this not be said to amount to the lowest-risk means of acquiring nuclear weapons?

Japan currently shoulders the ¥1 trillion annual cost of maintaining the US forces based in the country. Could that sum not be allocated as a contribution to NATO instead? That would be the point at which the Japan-US Security Treaty would be subsumed into NATO. Instead of that, Japan would be included in the "nuclear sharing" arrangement. (In fact, the idea of sharing nuclear weapons has been addressed at length by Shigeru Ishiba, the former Secretary-General of the ruling Liberal Democratic Party.) Apart from Russia, Japan has potential neighbouring enemies in the form of China and North Korea, and for the present probably needs around 300 nuclear warheads and bombs.

Of course, any limits on Japan's use of such armaments would not reside in the NATO Headquarters: as America is involved in NATO, if it said "No" to providing Japan with nuclear weapons, Japan would have to abide by it. If Germany wanted to deploy the nuclear weapons stationed there, it is possible that America would not easily agree to them being used to strike Russian territory. However, one should not compare this with the Japan-US Security Treaty, whose provisions appear worthless. It may be an extreme thing to say regarding the possession of actual nuclear warheads but, if Japan were to find itself in a truly critical situation, it might choose to use them in order to survive. Speaking without fear of misunderstanding, whatever America might do, if we only had nuclear weapons we would be far safer and more secure than now, when we have to rely on the meaningless Japan-US Security Treaty.

A nuclear capability in line with the constitution

Currently, in accordance with the three nuclear principles of neither possessing nor manufacturing nuclear weapons, nor permitting their introduction into Japanese territory, the received wisdom that Japan cannot acquire a nuclear capability holds sway, but this notion is absolutely wrong.

Despite the huge importance of this matter, it is not well known that, according to the Government's official view, Japan can equip itself with nuclear weapons while remaining in compliance with the current constitution. In 1957 the then-Prime Minister Nobusuke Kishi (Shinzo Abe's maternal grandfather) made a statement to the Diet, albeit delivered in prudent terms, that the constitution did not prohibit Japan's possession of nuclear weapons to the minimal extent necessary for its self-defence.

That is to say that Article 9 of the constitution can be interpreted along the lines that there is no problem in Japan possessing nuclear weapons as long as their number does not exceed the minimum required for self-defence. What is more, if Japan's conventional military capacity in the form of its Self-Defence Forces does not prove sufficient in guaranteeing the country's security, making up this shortfall with nuclear weapons accords with the constitution. Moreover, Hayato Ikeda, who succeeded Nobusuke Kishi, was of the view that the constitution allowed Japan to equip itself with nuclear weapons. As for the stance of other countries, having been ridiculed by French President Charles de Gaulle as "a transistor salesman", Prime Minister Ikeda bitterly reflected that Japan's ability to make itself heard would increase if it had such armaments.

When Prime Minister Eisaku Sato took office in 1964, he initiated moves towards acquiring nuclear weapons. With China having conducted a nuclear test just before the start of his administration, Mr Sato urged on US Ambassador Edwin Reischauer the need for Japan to become a nuclear power. The rattled American side tried to mollify him with a promise that its "nuclear umbrella" would "definitely" extend to the Far East, and an apparently reassured Prime Minister Sato was able to steadily reduce the cost of Japan's defence. Eventually, with the return of Okinawa in prospect, he went so far as to proclaim anew Japan's adherence to the "three non-nuclear principles" while avoiding any intemperate talk of Japan acquiring a nuclear capacity. Whereas the official line up to the time of the Ikeda cabinet had been "We have no immediate intention of acquiring nuclear weapons but that does not mean we cannot do so", in the Sato administration that was abruptly changed to the explicit declaration: "We can acquire nuclear weapons but choose not do so."

In 1968, the Agriculture Minister Tadao Kuraishi advocated Japan equipping itself with nuclear weapons as a matter of "common sense". Having expressed his personal opinion that "Japan, with its stupid constitution, lacks the basis for independent action", and voicing the wish that Japan could have atomic bombs and an army of 300,000 men, he made the common-sense proposal that Japan should acquire a nuclear capability. When he was pressed on this stance by the opposition parties in the Diet, Prime Minister Sato abruptly sacked him. Mr Sato went on to receive the Nobel Peace Prize for his "three non-nuclear principles", but in receiving a personal honour he was in fact blocking Japan's progress towards the acquisition of nuclear weapons.

Since then, just as Ambassador Reischauer had envisaged and based on a tacit agreement with Japan, US nuclear submarines and aircraft carriers abundantly stocked with atomic weapons have been calling at Japanese ports. As the three non-nuclear principles have famously been ignored, they should be quickly abandoned. Through a mere cabinet meeting, they could be shorn of any legal force. If the administration of the day had the courage to change direction, this issue could be rendered meaningless.

An independent nuclear capability

If joining NATO did not live up to its expectations, Japan could turn its attention to acquiring an independent nuclear capability. Japan has to bear an annual burden of ¥1 trillion to maintain the US military presence on the basis of the Japan-US Security Treaty, which offers absolutely no guarantee of protection. However, the US military presence amounts to a base for America rather than for Japan. Thus, spending that money on acquiring its own nuclear capability would seem to contribute far more to Japan's security.

As I have outlined, the greatest obstacle to Japan acquiring nuclear weapons is not in fact Article 9 of the constitution but the three nuclear principles, although the Treaty on the Non-Proliferation of Nuclear Weapons (NPT) amounts to another impediment. This pact forbids any countries other than

America, Russia, the UK, France and China from possessing nuclear weapons.

In 1993 North Korea withdrew from the NPT. India, Israel and Pakistan are non-signatories. The NPT is in fact a selfish arrangement but Japan has unfortunately ratified it, and the government would be contravening it if it were to discuss equipping itself with nuclear weapons. Thus, unless Japan were to withdraw from it, the government could not make public its deliberations on acquiring a nuclear capability.

Amid such restrictions, what can be done to pursue this goal? One idea is to promote the notion furtively. However, even if the Japanese Government were of a mind to develop such a strategy, it might not have the backbone to follow it through. Firstly, Japan's intelligence capacity is as porous as a bamboo basket, making the country "a paradise for spies". And as for the issue of greatest interest to the world's intelligence services, that is the development of nuclear weapons, a look at the case of Iran shows how difficult it is to maintain secrecy.

To return to the narrative, if one cannot address the matter furtively, there is nothing for it but to do so openly. One idea in this regard is for the issue to be taken up not by the government but in a research publication from a private-sector think tank. Of course, the think tank and its findings would carry a sense of government approval. As the first step towards the acquisition of nuclear weapons, would it not make sense to come up with a road map?

Germany's deliberations on hosting nuclear weapons

As discussed earlier, as a result of the nuclear sharing arrangement with NATO, there are said to be around 20 to 100 nuclear warheads installed in Germany, all of them aimed at Russia. The country can be regarded as already having reached the stage of equipping itself with such armaments, and discussion of the idea of developing them independently is not far off.

As a matter of fact, German defence spending is on a steadily rising trend. There is general agreement among the public on the need to modernise the country's military. At the same time, the deployment of military personnel overseas, something which used to attract considerable opposition, is under way to a noticeable extent. Against this backdrop, deliberations on an independent nuclear capacity for Germany have begun. As one reason for this, one can point to the strong confrontational stance towards NATO shown in recent years by Russian President Putin, which has triggered great alarm in Germany. Moreover, during the last US administration there was also the element of nervousness engendered by Donald Trump and his "America First" mantra.

In November 2016, Germany's most conservative newspaper, the Frankfurter Allgemeine Zeitung, penned these words in its editorial: "Concerning the momentous question over which Germans are agonizing, that is, 'Should Germany develop its own nuclear weapons?', we have to face up to the reality that, under President Trump, our security is at risk."

Then Roderich Kaisewetter, minister in charge of foreign affairs of the Christian Democratic Union, led by Chancellor Merkel, suggested a debate on Germany equipping itself with nuclear weapons, declaring the topic something which should not be regarded as taboo. As had been expected, Trump remarked: "NATO is obsolete. Its members need to bear more of the financial burden involved." Although Germany was supposed to benefit from the nuclear protection provided by NATO, in view of Trump's attitude towards the organisation, Germans could have been forgiven for concluding that they had no security at all.

With America seeking to cut its share of the NATO budget and even reduce the scope of the nuclear-sharing arrangement, there is also the issue of the UK, a nuclear power and a member of NATO, having left the EU and distanced itself somewhat from Continental Europe. As for France, it possesses nuclear warheads solely for possible use against Russia. Even in the east, Europe at present is incapable of standing up to Russia. In Germany current thinking rejects reliance on other countries, with debate having begun on linking up with Poland, which is also wary of Russia, and together developing an independent nuclear capacity.

Mr Kaisewetter, as mentioned earlier, reacting to Trump's words, took a step forward when he commented, "If America is not going to extend its 'nuclear umbrella' to Germany, then Germany and Europe should pursue their own nuclear deterrent." At the same time, the influential weekly magazine Der Spiegel published an article saying, "The time has come for Germany to consider developing its own nuclear weapons." I do not believe that Germany, notwithstanding Biden's more positive approach to NATO, would be willing to simply be dependent on the US's nuclear umbrella.

Back in 1969, Japan's Foreign Ministry held secret talks with diplomats of the then-West Germany exploring the possibility of acquiring a nuclear capability. Although little seems to have emerged as a result, the global environment has changed greatly since then. Like Japan, Germany was one of the losers of the Second World War, and in the United Nations both countries have been treated as enemies. The fact that Germany has at last begun to deliberate seriously on obtaining nuclear weapons may well prove to be the catalyst for altering the course of the debate in Japan. We need to look into ways of collaborating with Germany in this regard.

Chapter 2

Observations on the nuclear powers

At present there are nine countries possessing nuclear weapons, consisting of America, Russia, Britain, France, China, India, Pakistan, Israel and North Korea. Although Israel has never publicly admitted to having them, most specialists are of one mind that it is a nuclear power. How is it, then, that these countries have reached the point of possessing nuclear weapons?

Among these nine nations, America, Russia, Britain, France and China are the permanent members of the United Nations Security Council as a result of having been the victors of the Second World War. One might refer to this situation as "victors' privilege", but by virtue of their possession of nuclear weapons these countries have performed the role of upholders of the postwar regime. In fact, the United Nations reflects the influence of the Allied Powers that emerged victorious in the Second World War. It is an organisation designed to maintain the depressed world ranking of the losers in that conflict, Japan and Germany. Like outdated documents, even in the United Nations Charter Japan and Germany are still treated as "enemy countries". That is why, notwithstanding their status as the world's third- and fourth-largest economies, Japan and Germany are excluded by the permanent members of the UN Security Council.

Of course, even if one equates countries victorious in the war with those possessing nuclear weapons, it does not mean that all of the victors moved in unison to acquire such armaments. Directly after the Second World War, the Cold War began between the free nations centred on America and the Communist countries led by Russia. Moreover, with China's success in developing nuclear weapons in 1964, the People's Republic of China went on to replace the Republic of China (Taiwan) as a permanent member of the United Nations Security Council.

Reasons for the world's tacit acceptance of a nuclear-armed India

The Non-Proliferation Treaty accepts the special status of the five powers America, Russia (formerly the Soviet Union), Britain, France and China, which have already developed nuclear weapons, and forbids other countries from acquiring a similar capacity. Although this reflects the laudable aim of reducing the number of nuclear weapons and bringing about their elimination in the future, for the nuclear states it helped nurture their wish to perpetuate their military superiority. In these circumstances, India and Pakistan, motivated by a sense of unfairness, refused to ratify the treaty.

Their position was understandable given that, even though the nuclear powers were obliged by the Treaty to reduce their nuclear arsenals, America and the Soviet Union did not let up on their nuclear development rivalry, at one time increasing their stocks of warheads to over 20,000 each. Recently the US and Russia have reduced their arsenals, motivated mainly by the wish to cut costs rather than by altruism. (However, on 1 February 2019 the US broke the Intermediate-Range Nuclear Forces Treaty with Russia, which mirrored America's action the following day.) Meanwhile, since the NPT came into being, Britain, France and China have actually increased the numbers of nuclear warheads in their possession. Those countries recognised as nuclear powers under the NPT have absolutely no intention of giving up the privileges they acquired by virtue of their victory in the Second World War.

India's skilful exploitation of the international situation

In 1974 India, not a signatory of the NPT, having conducted a successful test, joined the ranks of the nuclear-armed states. But why had India sought to acquire nuclear weapons? And why had a country that was not a permanent member of the UN Security Council been allowed to do so?

The direct reason for India's determination to acquire a nuclear capability was the threat posed by China. In 1962 there was a major military confrontation between the two countries, who had frequently engaged in border skirmishes before. China overwhelmed India with its military might, inflicting on the latter a humiliating defeat. And not only that, two years later China conducted a successful test and became a nuclear power. Thereafter India was continually threatened by China, having its border violated and some of its land seized. Alarmed at this situation, India's leaders took the decision to equip the country with nuclear weapons.

However, in 1974, the year when India conducted its nuclear test, at a time when the NPT had already come into force, the country attracted considerable international criticism for refusing to sign up to the Treaty and for going ahead with the test regardless. In response the Indian Government insisted it had conducted a "peaceful nuclear explosion" for civilian purposes, although of course its intention was to divert the technology to military use.

Against the backdrop of India's sophistry there was the confrontation between the Soviet Union and China. As members of the Eastern camp, both countries were ranged against America and Europe, but from the latter half of the 1950s onwards, after

Khrushchev had criticised Stalin, their paths diverged and, with incidents such as the military clash on Damansky Island in 1969, relations deteriorated drastically. Those were the circumstances in which Soviet attention turned to India. It is not surprising that, from that time on, India developed a close relationship with the Soviet Union, receiving military and economic aid as well as benefiting from Soviet technology in its development of nuclear weapons. Moreover, if India had nuclear weapons, it would be able to navigate its hostile relations with China. As they say, "My enemy's enemy is my friend."

Meanwhile, America also assisted India in order to deter Chinese expansion. While publicly criticising India, America and the country's former colonial master Britain saw merit in there being in Asia a country that could stand up to the military might of the Soviet Union and China in the Eastern bloc. For that reason, although India was not publicly recognised as a nuclear power, there was tacit acknowledgement that it had gained such a status.

Tense relations with its neighbour an exacerbating factor

With India acquiring nuclear weapons, there was the factor of its historical antagonism with Pakistan. Though they had both been part of a British colony, at the time of independence the area mainly populated by Hindus became independent India and that with a Muslim majority acquired independence as Pakistan. However, because some regions such as Kashmir had mixed populations, there was rivalry as each country regarded them as its own, and against this backdrop the two countries fought their third war in 1971. The mutual hostility continues to this day, with occasional skirmishes.

At that time India, with one eye on China, conducted a nuclear test, resulting in Pakistan, the loser in their war, setting about developing atomic weapons. India reacted to this by pressing ahead with its own nuclear development programme.

In a forceful reaction to news of Pakistan's nuclear test in 1998, India embarked on another test of its own. Moreover, having made considerable progress, it dropped any secrecy surrounding its intentions, openly admitted its military ambitions and declared itself a nuclear power. Of course, at the same time it insisted that the nuclear capability it had acquired amounted to defensive weapons for its own security, which would only be used to the minimum extent possible to ensure that it was not subject to nuclear threats from other countries. In addition, it did its best to placate international public opinion with its promise not to conduct any more nuclear tests.

As might have been expected, India was unable to avoid international economic sanctions, but was otherwise unaffected. Ignoring criticism and sanctions from other countries, it continued to emphasise nuclear weapons as the basis for its security. Now, as we find ourselves in the 21st century, the way the world sees India has changed. Through its rapid economic growth, it has become a major player in the global economy.

With a population second only to China's in size, India represents an attractive market. In order to strengthen bilateral economic ties, in 2007 the India-United States Civil Nuclear Agreement was signed. It stipulated that, in exchange for US civilian nuclear technology, India would submit to inspections by the International Atomic Energy Agency (IAEA). However, as it was left to India to determine whether certain elements were for civilian or military use, the agreement amounted to acquiescence in its development of nuclear weapons. At the same time, India promised to cooperate with other countries concerning its nuclear programme. In short, however, it was the continued sharp rise in China's military spending that was the major factor behind America's decision to forge the agreement with India.

In 2008 the IAEA, having approved the contents of the agreement and publicly refraining from recognising India as a nuclear power, in fact declared India to be an exceptional case, which in effect amounted to acknowledging that it had nuclear weapons. Moreover, in September 2018 the first "2+2" meeting between the US and India (involving the two sides' foreign and defence ministers) took place, and the bilateral relationship, including a joint declaration on strengthening military ties, became closer.

Taking a firm stand against the nuclear threat from China and Pakistan, and convinced that a nuclear capacity was essential to rid itself of that danger, India was able to breach the monopoly of possession of nuclear weapons enjoyed by the victors of the Second World War. But where does that leave Japan? Faced with the nuclear weapons of North Korea and China, can it not come up with an effective solution? Our country's leaders have yet to come close to grasping the obvious answer.

The US needs a nuclear India to counter the nuclear powers of China and Pakistan. As China and North Korea are becoming increasingly aggressive, now is the time for a nuclear Japan to step up to the plate in standing up to them.

Pakistan makes its voice heard

With India having gone nuclear, Pakistan, its bitter rival since independence, was not about to stay silent. The reason why Pakistan did not sign up to the NPT was that India had refused to do so. With the possibility that India could acquire nuclear weapons, Pakistan could not take the risk of binding itself to the NPT.

Pakistan suffered a heavy defeat in its third war with India in 1971. A particularly serious blow was the loss of East Pakistan, which became the independent state of Bangladesh. Moreover, if India acquired nuclear weapons, there would be no chance of confronting it on equal terms. In 1974 Pakistan's Prime Minister Zulfikar Ali Bhutto declared: "If India threatens us with nuclear weapons, we will respond by acquiring our own even if we have to eat grass."

It was China that extended a helping hand to Pakistan. Whereas Pakistan had previously been close to America, the assistance the latter granted India brought Pakistan into China's orbit in view of their aligned interests regarding India. China furnished Pakistan with military and economic assistance, including plenty of support with the development of a nuclear capacity. Just as the Soviet Union was extending aid to India as a means of reining in China, so China began to assist Pakistan in order to put pressure on India.

The year 1979 turned out to be favourable for Pakistan's nuclear development efforts. That year the Soviet Union invaded Afghanistan, prompting the US to feel it was necessary to aid the anti-Soviet guerrillas to bring an end to the subjugation of the country. The US needed the cooperation of Pakistan in order to provide a conduit for that aid. And Pakistan was not inclined to offer its cooperation free. In return it sought military assistance. As the US was constrained by law from extending military assistance to countries pursuing nuclear development, it decided to feign ignorance of Pakistan's nuclear ambitions. Slowly but surely, Pakistan proceeded with its covert nuclear development programme and in 1998, having conducted a successful test, was able to take its place alongside the world's other nuclear powers.

Pakistan's nuclear test coincided with the end of the Cold War and the onset of the global movement against nuclear proliferation led by America and, along with India which had likewise conducted a nuclear test, it suffered the imposition of severe economic sanctions by the United Nations. However, events favoured Pakistan in the form of the multiple terrorist attacks that struck America in 2001.

Under the Taliban, Afghanistan became a sanctuary for al-Qaeda, the main player among the terrorists. In order to strike at them, America needed Pakistan's cooperation. For this reason, it had no option but gradually to ease the economic sanctions on Pakistan. With Pakistan receiving such treatment, it was necessary to extend to India the same benefit, which was one of the factors leading to the US-India agreement. Having thereby accorded India recognition for its nuclear status, would it not be necessary to make an exceptional case of Pakistan too?

Ultimately, this did not mean that either India or Pakistan at that time possessed long-range nuclear missiles that could reach America. The circumstances did not represent a direct threat to America. In the worst case, if a nuclear exchange suddenly occurred between India and Pakistan, they were in any case on the other side of the world. As there was little risk of America suffering direct harm, it seems to have just accepted the situation.

One can thus say that both India and Pakistan succeeded in acquiring nuclear weapons through their skilful exploitation of the international geopolitical circumstances. There seems much that Japan, shackled by the constraints of the NPT, can learn from the two countries' nuclear diplomacy. It is a matter for regret that Japan does not seem to have politicians who can exercise a diplomacy that similarly exploits the interests and motivations of the nuclear powers. If Japan seriously wants to stop the annexation of Taiwan by China, as PM Suga declared in the White House on 16 April 2021, it would be utterly irresponsible to suggest that, in its present state, Japan could play a role in holding the nuclear-armed Chinese military in check.

Israel and its adroit diplomacy

Israel can be counted as a country which definitely possesses nuclear weapons. Although it has never officially confirmed or denied this to be the case, it is generally reckoned to have more than 80 nuclear warheads. In fact, it has never acknowledged when it acquired such weapons, how many nuclear warheads it has, or even whether it actually possesses them or not.

However, in the past there was an occasion which led to the strong suspicion that Israel was engaged in nuclear development. That was what is known as the "Vela incident". On 22 September 1979, a "double flash" was detected in the atmosphere in the vicinity of the Prince Edward islands at a midway point south of the Cape of Good Hope and north of the Antarctic. The incident occurred in what was a very narrow area of that covered by the international observation network and was detected by an American Vela Hotel reconnaissance satellite.

A "double flash" consists of a first flash triggering nuclear fission and a second one as the nuclear explosion. A Vela Hotel satellite was equipped with special sensors which could discern evidence of a nuclear test on the basis of the Partial Nuclear Test Ban Treaty. Although the American Monitoring Committee failed to confirm what had happened, it was widely believed internationally that Israel and South Africa had jointly conducted an atmospheric nuclear test. Furthermore, the fact that Israel stubbornly refused to sign up to the Non-Proliferation Treaty despite being repeatedly requested to do so was another reason why it was suspected of possessing nuclear weapons.

Israel's circumstances at the time could perhaps be regarded as corroborating evidence. From the time of its establishment in 1948 the country had been in a perpetual state of conflict with the Arab nations, as seen from the Third Arab-Israeli War (the Six-Day War) with its neighbours in 1967 and the Fourth Arab-Israeli War (the Yom Kippur War) in 1973. Israel was faced with constant insecurity as, even though it had been consistently victorious on the battlefield, it faced unwavering hostility from its neighbours and never knew when it might be attacked again. It is scarcely surprising that, with its very survival at stake, it felt impelled to develop a nuclear capability.

Although Israel's possession of atomic weapons is now regarded as beyond question, the simple fact that it is assumed to have nuclear missiles is enough to make its enemies hesitate to mount an attack. On the other hand, if Israel admitted to having nuclear weapons, this would trigger a rush by the Arab countries to equip themselves with a similar capacity, for which it would not be able to escape international condemnation. This "strategy of vagueness" is a skilful and intriguing way of acquiring a nuclear capability.

But why was Israel able to develop nuclear weapons? The Soviet Union and China assisted the Arab countries, so its situation was different from that of India and Pakistan. However, many of the scientists engaged in nuclear physics research were Jewish and, having fled to America to escape persecution by the Nazis, led the way with the Manhattan Project. Some of them, once Israel had been founded, went back to live in the "mother country". In addition, from the consistently pro-Israel thrust of America's Middle East strategy, it is easy to imagine the progress the country achieved in its nuclear development. It is also said that Israel obtained the cooperation of France which, with its independent foreign policy distinct from that of the US and the UK, wished to regain its influence in the Middle East.

Furthermore, South Africa, with which it is said to have conducted a joint test, had once possessed nuclear weapons. In exchange for uranium, which South Africa produced, Israel reportedly provided technological assistance. As reasons for South Africa's nuclear capability, possible factors often cited include the international repulsion at its policy of apartheid, or white minority rule, its wish to intimidate the neighbouring black-ruled countries and their oppressed black citizens, the appearance of a succession of socialist countries in the surrounding region and the presence of Cuban forces in Angola.

Subsequently, along with the improvement in the security environment following the collapse of the Soviet Union and the abolition of apartheid, South Africa decided to abolish its nuclear weapons. In 1991 it signed up to the Nuclear Non-Proliferation Treaty and in 1993 announced the scrapping of its entire nuclear arsenal.

North Korea joins the club

Let us consider the case of North Korea, which became a nuclear power as recently as 2006. Its inability to force the surrender of South Korea in the Korean War and its experience of confronting the hostile South Korean and American forces at the 38th parallel seem to have made it strongly inclined towards the development of nuclear weapons. Gaining possession of a nuclear reactor from the Soviet Union as a condition of the cessation of hostilities, it of course ignored the promises it had made regarding its use of the technology for peaceful purposes and proceeded with a nuclear weapons development programme.

In 1993 North Korea announced its intention to withdraw from the Nuclear Non-Proliferation Treaty, leading to moves to reach a compromise with America. However, by that time its nuclear development had made considerable progress, as can be surmised by what is said to have been a decision by then-President Clinton to bomb the facilities from the air. There is no doubt about Pakistan's involvement in this progress, led by Professor Abdul Qadeer Khan, who, through his "underground nuclear network", sold technology for manufacturing nuclear weapons to Iran, Libya and North Korea. In 1998 Pakistan conducted two nuclear tests, but one of them is said to have been on behalf of North Korea. Then in 2003, when it is thought to have set the goal of manufacturing nuclear weapons, it declared once again that it was withdrawing from the Nuclear Non-Proliferation Treaty and in 2006 carried out a successful nuclear test.

America was very much aware that North Korea had become a nuclear power. The dictatorship's leaders were keenly aware of what had happened to Saddam Hussein as the despotic ruler of a non-nuclear state and were clearly determined not to follow that path. Meanwhile, in legal terms the Korean War was still under way and, with 290,000 American troops in place along the 38th parallel, they could have attacked North Korea at will. Moreover, the US forces in Japan would have been able to launch an aerial attack whenever they wished.

One might say that North Korea's rulers were struck with terror that they could be overthrown at any time. As I argue at the beginning of this piece, nuclear-armed states are in a position to wage war mercilessly on their non-nuclear counterparts. When it comes to conflict between countries which are both nuclear powers, however, the situation is quite different. That is the reality facing India, Pakistan, China, and Israel as well. That is why North Korea rushed headlong into the development of nuclear warheads and long- and short-range ballistic missiles as the sole means of ensuring its survival.

Japan seems blithely to believe that the "nuclear umbrella" provided by the Japan-US Security Treaty will protect it from an atomic attack by North Korea, but it needs to take to heart the reasons why the latter acquired a nuclear capability. This brings up the question of whether, in the event that North Korea were attacked by America, its allies China and Russia would seek to protect it by striking at America.

The fact is that, unlike Japan and the trust it places on the Japan-US Security Treaty, North Korea is not naïve enough to rely on China to come to its aid by confronting America. Quite the contrary. History shows that China has repeatedly invaded the Korean peninsula in order to exert its control. Thus, North Korea thinks that, if the US set about attacking it, China would use that as a pretext for intervening militarily and taking control of the whole country. The nightmare for China is a situation in which South Korea and America annihilated North Korea, bringing a US military base to its doorstep. In these circumstances it would not be surprising if China adopted the strategy of putting North Korea under the control of the Chinese Communist Party.

In military and geopolitical terms, the Korean peninsula is extremely important to China, on a par with Crimea's significance to Russia. If the Korean peninsula entered the American sphere of influence, there is the fear that the Chinese military, particularly the Navy, as well as encroaching on the Japanese archipelago as it is doing now, would block off the exit from the Yellow Sea, making it impossible for ships to freely navigate the Pacific Ocean. There is also the fact that China has tolerated North Korea's nuclear development as a breakwater. The sense of crisis would be the same for Russia as, if North Korea were subsumed into the US sphere of influence, that situation would be keenly felt in Vladivostok, the home port of Russia's Pacific fleet.

North Korea not dependent on China's nuclear prowess

In short, it is conceivable that North Korea could be attacked by America, China or even Russia. All of these scenarios would represent a crisis for the Kim family's control of the country. Therefore, North Korea does not depend on China's nuclear might or on Russia's. All it has to depend on are its own nuclear weapons.

North Korea is a country whose conduct is driven solely by the imperative to survive. In fact, it is a dictatorship in which the survival of the Kim family is enough. The late Kim Jong-il pressed ahead with the development of nuclear weapons on the premise that, no matter how much the economy suffered, simply having a nuclear capacity represented a victory. That is why he devoted a large portion of the national budget to nuclear development. Naturally, the domestic economy was in dire straits and the country barely managed to get by with assistance from its ally China, but one could say it was worth it as in 2006 Pyongyang managed a successful nuclear test. During that time one million of its citizens are said to have starved to death.

However, this fact was of no consequence for Kim Jong-il. Whereas for Japanese people the acquisition of a nuclear capacity in exchange for one million deaths through starvation would be regarded as a disaster, for Kim it was a great success. His determination to achieve nuclear armed status at whatever cost to his people had an identical outcome to the misery inflicted on the Chinese people by Mao Zedong.

So what about the current incumbent Kim Jong-un? His behaviour is exactly the same as his father's. It would be fine if such tyranny had triggered a revolt, but as suppressing complaints is an important element of the regime's survival it concentrates every effort on maintaining public order.

Nonetheless, people suspected of dissent are routinely sent to concentration camps or executed. For Kim Jong-il the economy is secondary to his acquisition of nuclear weapons. As for the negotiations he conducted with former US President Donald Trump, if they had produced a beneficial outcome, from the resulting resumption of diplomatic relations with Japan he would have received economic assistance in lieu of war reparations. In those circumstances Kim might have been able to emulate South Korea and the rapid recovery it achieved following the ravages of the Korean War, known as "the Miracle of the Hangang River".

The prospect of a nuclear domino effect in the Middle East

So far we have focused on the countries which currently possess nuclear weapons and how they came to acquire them, but we also need to look at those which seem likely to become nuclear powers. They are the Islamic Middle Eastern nations of Turkey, Saudi Arabia and Iran. Saudi Arabia and Pakistan have come to a secret agreement on nuclear technology. There is an understanding between them that, in an emergency, Pakistan would supply Saudi Arabia with atomic weapons. The agreement stipulates that the two countries are one in terms of nuclear defence and includes the concept of collective defence in an emergency.

Of course, both countries publicly deny that such an agreement exists, but it is an open secret that most of the funds needed for Pakistan's nuclear development programme have been provided by Saudi Arabia. In return, Pakistan is prepared to supply Saudi Arabia with nuclear weapons at any time.

As well as Saudi Arabia having been furnished with nuclear warheads that it can install on its fighter aircraft whenever it wishes, there are reports that it has secretly acquired medium-range ballistic missiles from China, meaning that the country is steadily moving towards becoming a nuclear power.

The backdrop to Saudi Arabia's urgent steps to acquire nuclear weapons is the hostility of a number of Arab countries towards not Israel but Iran. Although Saudi Arabia and Iran are both Islamic countries, they are engaged in a struggle for hegemony in the Persian Gulf region. Iran has long had ambitions to develop nuclear weapons and has been unable to conceal its headlong rush to become a nuclear power. If Shia Iran had atomic weapons, then of course Sunni Saudi Arabia would acquire them as well.

As for Turkey, as a member of NATO it hosts around 70 American strategic nuclear weapons, but President Erdogan has declared his wish to avoid relying on America and has moved closer to Russia. If Iran and Saudi Arabia acquired nuclear weapons, Turkey would respond by doing likewise. It might well withdraw from the Nuclear Non-Proliferation Treaty and procure atomic weapons from its fellow Muslim state, Pakistan.

Chapter 3

A nuclear capability and relations with the US

International background to Japan's acquisition of nuclear arms

Clearly, a nuclear capacity is indispensable for Japan, but the important thing is whether and when Japan could gain the acceptance of the global community for such a situation. As we said in Chapter 1, the most likely development is Japan joining NATO, but if this were not possible there would be no alternative to looking into the acquisition of an independent nuclear capability. However, to gain acquiescence for this both domestically and internationally, a change in the international situation would be necessary.

Ultimately, for Japan to acquire nuclear weapons would require a situation in which the world was facing a major crisis, there were widespread calls in Japan for a nuclear capability and the democratic elements of the international community, particularly the US, the UK and the EU, judged it to be in their interests for Japan to make such a move.

If we consider the current reality, it is clear that Japan does not have the approval of the US. As we saw in Chapter 2, the road for non-nuclear states to acquire an atomic capability is complicated, involving the acquiescence of those powers that have controlled the world since the end of the Second World

War in the form of the US, the UK and France, in other words the recognition of the nuclear powers through the Nuclear Non-Proliferation Treaty. Even if the nuclear powers ostensibly criticised such moves, the fact is that, if it reflected their international strategy and their pursuit of their own interests, no matter how much they professed to disapprove, history acknowledges them as nuclear powers. It is a case of "We can't help having them even though we don't really want them."

For instance, it is unthinkable that North Korea's acquisition of nuclear weapons did not have China's backing. If that were not the case, American missiles would have long since rained down on it and the Kim dynasty would have collapsed in the manner of Saddam Hussein in Iraq and Muammar Gaddafi in Libya. In fact, in 1994 former US President Bill Clinton seriously considered bombing North Korea but was constrained by China and abandoned that idea. As for China, there was a certain strategic value in having North Korea as a buffer zone between it and South Korea, in the freedom camp.

Meanwhile, America might well tacitly approve Japan's acquisition of nuclear weapons if it were for its own rather than Japan's benefit.

And such a situation is approaching. For evidence there is China's crackdown on Hong Kong in 2020 and its aggression in the South and East China Seas. Next will be its imposition of an actual Anti-Access/Area Denial situation over the Senkaku islands and the deployment of amphibious assault ships of its land, sea and air forces backed up by violent demonstrations by pro-China elements in Taiwan. In such an event it is possible that America will publicly broach the subject of a nuclear-armed Japan. In exchange for acknowledging China's "Hongkongification" of Taiwan, Japan will gain China's acquiescence for its acquisition of a nuclear capability.

Unless it faced an attack by China along the lines of that on Pearl Harbor, America would not have the appetite for an all-out war with China. This is because, in that event Russia would use that opportunity to make a move on the three Baltic states, Ukraine and Poland. America lacks the military might to take on both China and Russia at the same time. That makes China treating Taiwan in the manner of its crackdown on Hong Kong and Japan becoming a nuclear power a matter for negotiation between China and America. Meanwhile, Turkey, Saudi Arabia and Iran would probably acquire nuclear weapons. If China were convinced that Japan's nuclear weapons were not trained on it for a pre-emptive strike, it might well concentrate on unification with Taiwan.

The importance of Okinawa to Japan and the US

In this discussion Okinawa is the key. In confronting a situation in which China had given Taiwan the Hong Kong treatment and the Chinese Communist Party had taken direct control of the island, a nuclear-armed Okinawa would be indispensable to Japan and the US.

Furthermore, Okinawa, situated right in the middle of the Acheson Line, is the lynchpin in the projection of American power in the Pacific. Created by US Secretary of State Dean Acheson during the administration of President Harry S. Truman as the line of defence against communism, it is a line connecting the Aleutian Islands, the Japanese archipelago, Taiwan, the Philippines and Australia. If one looks at it on a terrestrial globe, it should be clear that Okinawa is in the middle of it. What is more, Okinawa is at the crossroads on the route linking Hawaii with the Persian Gulf in the Middle East. In short, it is no exaggeration to say that Okinawa, with its role at the heart of American global strategy and providing a base for the US military, from which its troops can be dispatched rapidly all over the world, helps give the US its hegemonic status.

In fact, Okinawa's importance to America is not just something that began recently. Having prevailed in the Mexican-American War, in 1848 the US took possession of California on the West Coast and secured the excellent port of San Francisco. It set the explicit goal of establishing trade links with China from there and making Japan a transit base in that regard. Then, under the orders of President Fillmore, Commodore Perry's fleet arrived in Japan. That was the arrival of "the Black Ships" in 1853.

Before Perry's ships reached Japan, they docked at Naha in Okinawa. Perry visited Sho Tai, the last king of the Ryukyu Kingdom, at Shuri Castle and declared his wish to open commercial links, but his actual aim was to take possession of the territory. For America, having approached from the northern part of the Pacific, there was a need to resist encroachment by Britain, which had established bases near the Chinese mainland from the West, that is to say Singapore, Hong Kong and the northern part of the island of Borneo. In that sense, Okinawa was an excellent location.

Perry visited Okinawa five times and, judging Nago Wan Bay, Unten Port, Taira Wan Bay, Kimbu Wan Port and Nakagusuku Bay to be suitable bases for his ships, carried out exhaustive surveys of the ocean, including such aspects as the depth of the water in the ports. On the basis of these surveys, he obtained sea charts covering the whole coastline of Okinawa as well as shipping maps and carried out preliminary work so that bases for his ships could be constructed at any time. Since then, Okinawa has been a historically important base for America's strategic and geopolitical relations with China.

Supposing for a moment that the Japan-US Security Treaty did not exist, America would defend Okinawa with all its might as it viewed it as its own territory but would probably expect the inhabitants of the rest of Japan to take care of their own security. However, losing Japan would entail losing Okinawa as well. This must be the dilemma that America faces. Thus, crude as it may sound, this could be the "trump card" to gain America's acquiescence in Japan becoming a nuclear power.

Exploiting China's preoccupations

In the event of Japan deciding to acquire a nuclear capability, there would clearly be a fierce response from China and Russia. For China, however, American and Japanese efforts to prevent its naval forces from passing through the Taiwan Strait because of its "Hongkongification" of Taiwan would be a problem. The fact that China would be concentrating on cleansing Taiwan of pro-independence elements would make it difficult to direct its energy to opposing the nuclearisation of Japan. Thus, instead of resisting that development, Japan and America, observing the reality of China's imposition of a Hong Kong-style outcome on Taiwan, would be able to negotiate with China on the basis of the actual situation prevailing at the time. Accordingly, America, making use of Japan's nuclear and financial resources, would in the long term have nuclear warheads aimed at China's throat.

As Xi Jinping has actually declared that Japan would not flinch from war if it acquired nuclear weapons, he may well be weighing up Taiwan and a nuclear-armed Japan. There is no doubt that he would choose China's absorption of Taiwan over war with Japan.

Chapter 4

Thoughts on what it really means to have atomic weapons

The reasons for acquiring a nuclear capability

If a country had nuclear weapons with the intention of changing the order in East Asia, it would of course be an erroneous policy. However, Japan's acquisition of nuclear weapons, rather than being part of an attempt to change the situation in East Asia, is something which ought to be considered on the basis of a defensive strategy as a means for the country's survival once US forces had withdrawn from East Asia and the region were undergoing major change. In this regard, let us consider the case of Israel. It is not that Israel is trying to change the situation in the Middle East through its possession of nuclear weapons. Rather, when all is said and done, they amount to a nuclear deterrent. Having nuclear weapons and displaying a willingness to retaliate if attacked is the most effective way of avoiding war.

Rather, one could say that Japan's possession of nuclear weapons would be a means of maintaining the balance of security in East Asia. So far America, as the self-appointed "world's policeman", has been able to prevent the military hegemony in East Asia of a rising China. However, a look at world history should show the absolute truth of the adage that a financial discrepancy amounts to a gap in the balance of power and that declining financial strength equates to weakening military power. It seems inevitable that China will impose a Hong Kong-style solution on Taiwan and that America will gradually withdraw from East Asia in the relatively near future. With 50,000 US military personnel currently stationed in South Korea and 20,000 in Japan, it is clear that the US lacks the financial resources to maintain such a large presence in the region if that included facing a Communist Taiwan. Thus somebody needs to make up the shortfall caused by the gradual reduction of the US presence and, if one considers the current national capacities of the various countries in Asia, the only one that could just about take on this role would be Japan.

In this sense, there is a link between America's gradual withdrawal from East Asia and Japan's adoption of a nuclear capacity. For America, this would amount to a timely rescue. For China, it would facilitate its subjugation of Taiwan in the manner of Hong Kong.

Renewed reflections on the importance of military power

In 1853 Commodore Perry's fleet docked in Uraga, with huge warships the like of which Japanese people in the Edo period had never seen and guns whose deafening blast terrified the locals. The following year Perry returned and signed the Japan-US Treaty of Amity with representatives of the Tokugawa Government. Reluctantly, the Bakufu found itself with no option but to bring to an end its policy of isolation. This was undoubtedly a case of "gunboat diplomacy".

Four years later, in 1858, Japan concluded Treaties of Amity and Commerce with Holland, Britain, France, Russia and the United States. But they were unequal treaties as, after its prolonged period of isolation, Japan had no sense of its place in an international context and there were no provisions for matters such as Japan's consular and judicial rights or autonomy concerning taxation. Moreover, through the military engagements with Britain, France, Holland and the United States for control of the Shimonoseki Straits in 1863 and 1864, Japan was left in no doubt about the discrepancy between its military prowess and that of the foreign powers. The Meiji Government keenly felt the gulf with the great powers, particularly the huge shortfall in Japan's military capacity. For that reason, it embarked on a course of speedy modernisation whatever the obstacles, and diligently set about boosting national prosperity and building up the military. Thus it was that in 1914 it succeeded in having all of the unequal treaties annulled. With victories in wars with China and Russia, Japan's military strength was no longer the object of derision. The emphasis placed by the Meiji Government on building a prosperous country and a powerful military was driven by the imperative of Japan's survival on the global stage.

Even today, that principle has hardly changed. It is only countries possessing substantial military power, and particularly those with nuclear weapons, that can look forward with confidence. This is true even for a small, impoverished state like North Korea.

Nuclear weapons alone will not produce a great power

In 2018 the well-known French thinker Emmanuel Todd visited Japan, where he advocated Japan possessing nuclear weapons as a matter of course. He insisted they should be for the defence of one's own country and ridiculed the idea of relying on a nuclear umbrella provided by others.

Those words echo my own thinking. Why do the Japanese people naïvely believe in such things as the Japan-US Security Treaty?

Todd also said: "Several years ago, when visits to the Yasukuni Shrine by the Japanese prime minister became a contentious issue, this is what I thought: Rather than the Japanese people or the Japanese prime minister talking about or engaging in visits to that shrine, would it not be better to concentrate on equipping themselves with real military power?"

He gave frank expression to my idea that national defence should be considered in a scientific way. The pros and cons of having a nuclear capability are not something to be addressed with a sentimental argument on the part of the victim of the atomic bombing. That would in a sense be irresponsible. It is incumbent on people who adopt an anti-nuclear stance to explain in scientific and rational terms how non-nuclear states are supposed to defend themselves against countries that are ready to use such weapons to attack others.

When an attempt is made to expound on the necessity of a nuclear capacity for Japan, a clamour is raised among those who, without properly investigating what this actually means, warn of a return to militarism and to the situation prevailing before WWII. However, simply having nuclear weapons does not mean a revival of Imperial Japan. In short, we are talking about a small, upright country being at the starting point of a process essential for its survival.

For Japan, vitality and prosperity will not be realised through revision of the constitution. When the Japanese people take on board the need for their country to become like the Venice of old, through the development of the newest and most powerful weapons, that is to say by using the power of science, then Japan may well become "a normal country" while avoiding the pitfalls of forgetting about science that so concerned the Showa Emperor Hirohito.

www.ingramcontent.com/pod-product-compliance
Lightning Source LLC
Chambersburg PA
CBHW022132280326
41933CB00007B/662